OTHER WORLDS AND BUDDHISM

The Three Spheres of Existence

Ananda L. Sirisena

Copyright ©Ananda L. Sirisena 2019

**Dedicated to my parents
Mr. P.H. & Mrs. M.S. Sirisena
who
taught their children to respect all
the religious beliefs of the world**

The author can be contacted by email on:

anandals@aol.com

Associated with the same author

One of the authors of:
"THE CASE FOR THE FACE - Scientists Examine The Evidence for Alien Artefacts On Mars" -
Adventures Unlimited, 1998

A researcher for the book: **"UFOs - THE EXTRATERRESTRIAL MESSAGE" - by Richard Lawrence.**
Cico Books, 2010

Author of:
"MASSIVE VIMANA (UFO) OVER THE ATOMIC WEAPONS ESTABLISHMENT - A Challenge for Parliament" - 2018
Available from Amazon Books

"Three things that cannot be hidden: the Sun, the Moon, the Truth" - attributed to the Buddha

Buddhist cosmology explained and expanded, in the light of modern scientific discoveries by the National Aeronautics Space Administration (NASA), the European Space Agency (ESA) and other space agencies - with reference to ancient texts.

(Cover picture courtesy of NASA)

Contents

Chapter	Page
1 - The Three Spheres	11
2 - Levels within the Spheres	16
3 - The Fine-Material Sphere	27
4 - Longevity and Epochs	41
5 - The Formless Sphere	65

INTRODUCTION

Buddhism as a religion has never denied the existence of extraterrestrial life.

SETI, the Search for Extraterrestrial Intelligence has been promulgated on radio SETI (rSETI), a search - listening on many frequencies and bandwidths for radio signals from outer space.

There is now a new and emerging scientific concept: pSETI, or planetary SETI. This new idea was introduced by emeritus professor Stanley V. McDaniel, philosopher, of Sonoma State University, who founded SPSR - the Society For Planetary SETI Research.

This new science is based on a search of planetary surfaces, including our Moon, for possible signs of extraterrestrial intelligence and its intervention on Mars or Venus, our nearest planetary neighbours, or any planet or moon in our solar system. A website link to SPSR can be found at:

http://spsr.nmcc.edu

This book hearkens back to the time of the Lord Buddha, also known as Prince Siddharta Gautama, who explained that there are many different types of abode (world) and many levels of consciousness throughout the Cosmos and elucidated on our place, i.e. the human point of sentience, in a seemingly vast and endless universe.

The Buddha lived, according to most scholars, from 563 - 480 BCE. (Others claim that he was born in 623 BCE and lived to 543 BCE.) A true historical figure lived in northern India with a ministry of over 40 years, during which time he travelled throughout the subcontinent and disseminated great wisdom and knowledge, based on his meditations on the human condition, human suffering and the human place in a universe of multiple realms, with varying mental conditions and levels of consciousness on each plane of existence.

His teachings were part of the acclaimed Eastern religious philosophy, in contradistinction to the Western Greek writings and philosophies of well known scholars such as Plato, Pythagoras and Aristotle.

The Buddha espoused knowledge about the cosmos which is gradually being proven today, by the latest scientific discoveries.

It is astonishing to think that over 2,500 years ago - before the advent of modern science, the Buddha spoke of "thousand-fold world systems". The word "thousand-fold" should be considered symbolic rather than an actual count. The Eastern Vedic writings and the main religious system of his time, namely Brahminism, also referenced other-worldly beings and life from elsewhere, as well as the word *"vimana"*, which also means 'mansion'.

Vimana refers to "aerial vehicle" as described in the Vedas. It appears to describe a flying ship, or a flying object, well before the advent of modern science and aeroplane flights.

THE THREE SPHERES OF EXISTENCE

CHAPTER 1

THE THREE SPHERES OF EXISTENCE

Buddhist texts have many references to the vastness of the Cosmos and the multiplicity of inhabitants that can be found in it.

The cosmology of Buddhism is founded on the expansive, ego-less premise that the physical, human plane of existence is only one of many.

One of the Buddhist texts, the Anguttara Nikaya, states:

"Kingship on Earth is a beggarly existence in comparison with the joys of the heavenly worlds"

The word "Nikaya" refers to a collection of discourses. The literal translation of "Anguttara" is 'factors beyond'.

It is the heavenly worlds - heavenly realms with lofty levels of supramundane tiers of evolved consciousness that we shall study in this book.

A very detailed exposition of moral and immoral thoughts, deeds and actions, (including speech) will be boiled down in the simplest diagrams, indicating 31 steps to a meditative reality - surpassing physical manifestation. The only absolute reality in Buddhism is termed: "Nirvana" (in Sanskrit) or "Nibbana" (in the sacred language of Pali). Nirvana is the *summum bonum* of Buddhist philosophy.

The Buddha himself made many references to the heavenly worlds, although he did not analyse in too much great detail conditions upon them, nor did he state whether any of the planets in our solar system corresponded to any of these higher types of worlds.

Human conceit is surely castigated by the knowledge that the human-type world is but fifth from the bottom rung of the cosmic ladder of spiritual evolution. We would be advised not to consider ourselves the only or the greatest living beings in the cosmos.

The Anguttara Nikaya (IV, 429) gives us a concept of time which is familiar to astronomers, cosmologists and science fiction writers of today: time is not the same everywhere.

"Fifty Earth years are equivalent to one day and night in one of the heavenly worlds, while in another a day and night is equivalent to no less than 1,600 Earth years."

(Anguttara Nikaya, Book of Fours)

The world systems of Buddhism are never static. They are in the process of either evolution or dissolution. Buddhist philosophy emphasises that nothing which is *manifest* or has been *manifested* in the past - physical, mental or psychic can remain static, for all is in a state of flux and impermanence. Future manifestation likewise must be in a constant flux. All manifestation is changing continuously, therefore cannot be regarded as absolute reality, only as mundane reality.

Such change applies to human and animal growth, blood flow, ageing processes, revolutions of thousands of worlds and moons and indeed everything we perceive and study in the universe, through our sensory inputs.

"As far as these suns and moons revolve, shedding their light in space, so far extends the thousand-fold world-system. In it are a thousand suns, a thousand moons, thousands of earths and thousands of heavenly worlds. This is said to be the thousand-fold minor world system."
                    Anguttara Nikaya, I.227.228)

Not all life forms on these world systems are likened to the biped human frame. A classification in the Anguttara Nikaya portrays several classes of living beings:

"The no-footed, the two-footed, the four-footed, the many-footed, those having or lacking material form, the conscious, the not-conscious and the super conscious."
                    (Anguttara Nikaya, III,35)

It seems that humanity needs to be prepared to encounter many different life forms as we travel out into interplanetary space and eventually explore the nearest parts of our Milky Way galaxy. Meeting extraterrestrial life forms will be both exciting and maybe even a little daunting.

We have been forewarned so we can prepare ourselves. The whole of terrestrial cultures can be educated to eventually meet with and have exchange of ideas with more advanced races who may or may not be hostile to us. It is said that on Earth when so-called "civilised" nations interacted with "non-developed" tribes there was a negative effect on the colonised peoples.

That need not be the case now as we can train ourselves to accept and understand more advanced, more intelligent species, no matter where they come from. Hollywood movies have probably taken these concepts to an extreme entertainment scenario but we do know the difference between fiction and fact.

CHAPTER 2

LEVELS WITHIN THE SPHERES

Formless sphere	ARUPA LOKA (4 levels)
Fine-material sphere	RUPA LOKA (16 levels)
Sense-desire sphere	KAMA LOKA (11 levels)

[Table 1]

The word "loka" generally means world.

Rupa = form,
Arupa = formless.

So the fine-material sphere is inhabited by beings of a higher order who still retain a form. There are said to be exceptions as we will see later.

Kama = sense-desire. This word "kama" must not be confused with 'kamma' (Sanskrit - 'karma' - action), which is a reference to the law of cause and effect - the karmic law which ensures that "one sows what one reaps". So the Kama Loka are levels of consciousness wherein the dwellers react to their senses and generate desires, either for the good of all or not, as each case must be self-judged.

The human type world is said to reside in the bottom sphere, the sense-desire category. There are said to be 11 levels of consciousness in the lower sphere. The fine-material sphere (Rupa loka) is said to contain 16 levels of high consciousness planes and 4 are described in the highest sphere of Arupa loka.

The total number of levels of consciousness, in the three spheres, is therefore 31 (4 + 16 + 11) We can now breakdown each sphere, detailing a "ladder of evolution" as it were, starting with the lowest sphere, the Kama Loka, then expanding to the Rupa Loka and eventually identifying the four levels of consciousness which constitute the formless sphere - the Arupa Loka.

OTHER WORLDS AND BUDDHISM - The Three Spheres of Existence

Abode type level	THE SENSE-DESIRE SPHERE (KAMA LOKA) - bottom sphere	
	THE DEVA LOKAS	
	Happy states	Life span in celestial years - C.Y. *
11	Devas utilising the Creations of others	16,000 C.Y.
10	Devas enjoying their own creations	8,000 C.Y.
9	Tusita devas (happy dwellers)	4,000 C.Y.
8	Yama devas	2,000 C.Y.
7	Realm of the thirty-three devas	1,000 C.Y
6	Realm of the four guardian kings	500 C.Y
	The lower states	
5	**Human world**	No limit
4	World of demons	No limit
3	Worlds of unhappy spirits	No limit
2	The animal world	Limited
1	Realms of the four hells	No limit

[Table 2]

* C.Y. - Celestial Year is defined approximately as 18,250 Earth years (based on a statement that one Celestial Day is equal to 50 Earth years)

Thus one Celestial Year = 50 x 365 = 18,250 Earth years.
Therefore, 500 CY = 9,125,000 Earth years and more, approximately.

The life span of beings on Level 11 (Devas utilising the creation of others) can be calculated as 292 million years. The calculation is a follows: 16,000 x 18,250 = 292,000,000.

Such long life spans may be mind-boggling to some - however in a universe with no known space-time boundaries and of inestimable age with any degree of accuracy, 288 million years in a cosmos said to be 13.7 billion years old, according to the Big Bang Theory, is but a twinkling fraction of time, a mere 2 per cent of the supposed age of the cosmos.

Teacher of gods and men

One of the titles given to the Buddha and readily accepted by him as being correct was that of a "Teacher of Devas and men".

The word deva (pronounced *they-vah*) is derived from the Sanskrit word *div* - to shine. It is cognate with the Latin word *deus*. So a deva is a 'shining being', a being from a higher level of consciousness or world.

Notice, from the Table above that Levels 6 - 11 are known as the Deva Lokas. Although Level 5, the human world is not classed as a Deva Loka, humans of high worldly status, such as kings, queens, princes, princesses and ministers, can also be called *devas* by convention and under certain circumstances. Also, quite a lot of Western occult writings, such as from the Theosophical Society or the Aetherius Society, refer to a class of nature spirits as the "*devic kingdom*", a term derived from the word deva.

Notice also, that although no time limit is imposed on the life span in the human world, at the present time we are said to have a very short life span. It is evident, from an incident mentioned in the Anguttara Nikaya, that the Buddha made direct reference to the three spheres of existence when explaining the process of rebirth.

He speaks of the "Sphere of Sense-Existence (Kama Loka)", a "Fine-Material Sphere (Rupa Loka) and an "Immaterial Sphere, or Formless Sphere (Arupa Loka)".

The Buddha said,

"Karma is the field, consciousness is the seed and craving is the moisture. Of beings hindered by ignorance and fettered by craving, their consciousness takes a hold in a lofty sphere, intermediate sphere or a lower sphere."

(Anguttara Nikaya, III,76)

It must be understood that none of these spheres, with their different levels of consciousness and varying psychic and mental abilities are said to be eternal. They are all subject to the vagaries of time and the very long life spans do come to an end in order for beings to evolve to another level.

The Buddha explained that beings are hindered by their own ignorance. If their lives are fettered by craving, then their consciousness, upon demise of one life, will result in a move to another level. Whether a life stream goes to a higher or lower plane depends upon their actions and accrued karma.

There are many other references in the Buddhist texts to the three Spheres of conscious existence. Sentient beings are said to be above animals and capable of understanding the Law of Karma, which is something that animals - without developed speech and high mentality - would be incapable of grasping. Action and reaction are equal and opposite says the Law. Many scholars draw a parallel with the biblical saying, "As you sow, so shall you reap."

Understanding the law of Karma is part and parcel of understanding the cycle of rebirth. The human type worlds sit midway in the sense-desire sphere (Kama Loka), wherein beings with mixed karma are reborn until they have striven spiritually to raise themselves above "Samsara" - the continuous wheel of birth, death and rebirth. Such striving is based on understanding the Law and developing mental control through meditation and attempting to remove constant craving and desire.

Abode type number 9, the Tusita Deva Loka is of some significance to Buddhists. Traditional belief is that the Buddha descended to Earth from the Tusita level. The planet Earth is only one example of a human-type abode and Buddhist texts do not identify any *specific* planet in our solar system, or outside our solar system, with these layers of consciousness.

It is clear that the lower five levels of consciousness are not mutually exclusive. On our planet, the animal kingdom forms part of the essential cycle of nature and cohabit the same terrain that we do. Indeed, we have successfully domesticated many type of animals who display certain commendable characteristics, like the loyalty displayed by dogs to their masters. Even though animals have mental limitations, they have similar physiological attributes such as breathing, feeling of pain, hunger pangs and even a sense of loneliness. Careful thought reveals that even though humans and animals reside on the same planet, we possess a different "level of consciousness" from the animals around us.

Likewise, we should be able to grasp that the different levels within the three spheres of existence maybe different levels of consciousness with much more variance than that displayed between animals and humans.

An essential lesson from this is that although physically humans and animals occupy the same physical plane on the same physical planet, the civilisations they produce and uphold are psychologically worlds apart, due to the colossal mental differences between humans and animals. *Homo sapiens sapiens* have developed complex speech as part of civilisation. Similarly there must be a vast difference between the human realm and say, the highest Brahma realms.

An interesting thought that can arise from this discussion is whether other worlds have similar wild, or domesticated animals. Are there worlds without animals? Or are there worlds with only animals?

It is clear that these world-types are not mutually exclusive. In a similar manner say the Buddhist texts, the differences between the thirty-one types of abode lie in consciousness levels rather than in an absolute physical or objective reality. All perceived types of worlds are still part of manifestation and are part of a *mundane reality* as understood by the sense organs and conscious interpretation by the human brain - which is the receptacle for sensory input.

This accentuates the teaching that all worlds, including the heavenly worlds, are evolving or dissolving in aeons of cosmic time. Buddhism teaches that the many planes of existence, as well as the thirty-one types of abode in space are a resultant of consciousness tied to karmic origination, even if life spans are said to be truly long, as measured in terms of Earth time.

The inhabitants of the middle sphere (Rupa Loka or Fine-Material Sphere) are referred to as Brahmas, to distinguish them from:
(i) the Devas of the Lower Sphere (Kama Loka or Sense-Desire Sphere) and

(ii) the more evolved Devas of the Higher Sphere (Arupa Loka or Formless Sphere)

Readers can refer to Table 1 to better grasp the Buddha's description of the higher planes.

THE PALI CANON

The teachings of the Buddha are preserved in three baskets (*tipitaka)*:

Vinaya Pitaka
Sutta Pitaka
Abhidhamma Pitaka

The first one deals with rules for monks and nuns and has 3 books.

The second one presents the moral and ethical code for successful human living and contains five *nikayas*..

The third one, from which much of the material for this book is drawn from, deals with the results of thoughts, words and actions combining to give birth on different planes with different levels of consciousness.

CHAPTER 3

The Fine-Material Sphere

The Fine-Material Sphere is known as Rupa Loka because the word "Rupa" means "material form", although it too has many other meanings dependent upon the context in which it is used. Older languages did not have the large vocabulary that our scientific disciplines have today. The sparse vocabulary meant that the same word was used in many different contexts and one needed to understand the context in which the word was used in order to make sense of the sentences and the meaning they were trying to elucidate upon.

The reason that the intermediate sphere is known as the Fine-Material Sphere is because it is said that the "matter" which forms the bodies upon these worlds is of a subtler nature than those in the Sense-Desire Sphere.

	THE FINE-MATERIAL SPHERE (RUPA LOKA)	
	Pure Brahma Abodes	
27	World of Supreme Brahmas	
26	World of Clear-Sighted Brahmas	FOURTH
25	World of Beautiful Brahmas	JHANA
24	World of Serene Brahmas	PLANE
23	World of Immobile / Durable Brahmas	
	Lower Brahma Abodes	
22	World of Sensationless/Consciousnessless Brahmas	
21	World of Greatly-Rewarded Brahmas	
20	World of Brahmas of Steady Aura	THIRD
19	World of Brahmas of Infinite Aura	JHANA
18	World of Brahmas of Minor Aura	PLANE
17	World of Radiant Brahmas	SECOND
16	World of Brahmas of Infinite Lustre	JHANA
15	World of Brahmas of Minor Lustre	PLANE
14	World of Great Brahmas	FIRST
13	World of Ministers of Brahmas	JHANA
12	World of Retinue of Brahmas	PLANE

[Table 3]

The sixteen abodes of the Fine-Material Sphere, 27 to 12 (see Table) are designated into two classes. The worlds from 27 to 23 are known as the Pure Brahma Lokas. The world-types from 22 to 12 are known as the Lower Brahma Lokas.

The Pali word "Brahma", as used in the Buddhist texts refers to "Gods", not a single supreme deity and does not have the same meaning as the Sanskrit word as used in the religion of Hinduism.

All beings in Abodes 1 to 27 are said to have a material body with an attached consciousness, albeit a fine-material body in the Rupa Lokas. A strange exception to this is said to be Abode Type 22, which is considered to be the habitat of beings having a material body but with their consciousness in a state of temporary suspension. The reasons for this are said to be somewhat complex but rebirth there is supposed to result from a particular type of concentrative contemplation and a deep meditation. This level is known as the World of Sensationless or Consciousnessless Brahmas.

Without a doubt, the Buddha made direct reference to the Deva and Brahma worlds in discourses to his disciples. In an exposition about psychic powers, the Buddha states:

"What now is the miracle of magic?
"There is one who enjoys the various kinds of magical power: having been one, he becomes many; having been many, he

becomes one; he appears through walls, enclosures and mountains as though in open space.

"He dives in and out of the Earth as if it were water. Without sinking he walks on water as if on earth. Seated cross-legged he travels through the sky like a winged bird. With his hand he touches and strokes the Sun and Moon, which are so mighty and powerful. Even as far as the Brahma worlds he wields mastery with his body."

(Anguttara Nikays, III. 60)

In two discourses in the text, the Digha Nikaya, the Lord Buddha describes how he encountered, whilst in a trance state, a being of radiant form, who had been suffering from the delusion that he was "The Almighty Brahma, the Most High, the Invincible One, the Preserver, Controller and Father of All that was and will be." The Buddha corrected his false and ignominious viewpoint.

In a sermon about anger, the Buddha advises:

"**One should speak the truth,**
"**One should not be angry,**

"One should give from scanty store to him who asks.
"By these three ways, one may go to the presence of the Devas."

(Dhammapada, 17.4)

In a direct and straightforward statement about the causes for the origination of *karma*, the Buddha says:

"It is not through actions (karma) born of greed, born of hate, born of delusion, that there is appearance of celestial beings (Devas), of humans or of any other creatures belonging to happy forms of existence (Brahmas); it is rather beings of the hells, of the animal kingdom, the ghostly realms or any others of a miserable form of existence that makes their appearances through actions born of greed, hate and delusion."

(Anguttara Nikaya, VI.39)

Notice that in this discourse the Buddha states that actions born out of greed, hatred or delusion result in unhappy states of life. Normally, human existence is "conditioned" by the Law of Kamma, therefore there is suffering on Earth - but the point made here is that such suffering need not exist, providing correct action is undertaken by humans in their everyday lives.

Buddhist texts contend that in the forty-five years between the Buddha's Enlightenment and his Pari-Nirvana, beings from the Deva Lokas and Brahma Lokas came to him for religious instruction. That is why the Buddha was addressed as a *"Teacher of Gods and Men"*.

One of the texts declares that forty-five terrestrial years correspond roughly to twelve hours in the life of a Deva from Abode-type number 7 (see table above) where the *life-span* of beings, on average is said to be one thousand of their years. So 24 hours in such a being's life would be equivalent to ninety of our terrestrial years on our physical plane. Ironically, ninety years can be a typical life span on our Earth for many of the current population throughout the world.

If ninety Earth years make one day on this type of world, their life-span can be calculated to be thirty-six and a half million terrestrial years, assuming of course that their year also has 365 days. But we know from studies of the planets in our Solar system, that different planets have different rotations on their own axes. So today we know that a year on different planets is not always 365 days.

In the first part of this study, we calculated life-spans on the Deva Lokas to be based on the simple equation that fifty Earth years make one celestial day. Should this cause confusion in the reader's mind, we need to remember that different texts present different figures for the average life-span. The point here is that on the higher types of world outlined in Buddhist cosmology, life-spans are in the thousands, hundreds of thousands or millions of our years. This may sound extraordinary to begin with but when one considers that today's science estimates the age of the cosmos to be billions of years, then it may not sound absurd at all.

On the higher Brahma worlds, the ages to which residents live are said to be incalculable in terrestrial terminology. Their longevity may cover several cycles of cosmic revolution - cycles during which whole worlds evolve and then dissolve back into the cosmos. Such cycles are called "Kalpas" in Sanskrit and "Kappas" in the sacred language of Pali. A loose translation of *kalpa* would be aeon.

The imparting of holy teaching by the Buddha to Devas and Brahmas from other worlds can only have been possible because of an elasticity of time. A telescopic adaptation of time consciousness, to conform to the time-frame of Earth during the Buddha's life would have enabled him to be a successful teacher of Gods and men.

As an illustration, let us compare the two neighbouring planets of Earth, Mars and Venus, in their rotation periods (around their own axes) and their revolution periods around our Sun.

Planet	Rotation	Revolution
Venus	243 days	224.7 days
Earth	1 day	365.26 days
Mars	1.03 days	1.88 years

[Table 4]

The days and years used in the above illustration are terrestrial days and years, our day being approximately 24 hours and our year being approximately 365 days. So we see that our time-frame is based on the rotation of Earth around its own axis (24 hours or 1day) and the time Earth takes to revolve around the Sun, one year. These figures are stated to be approximate because we also have to take into account that the Earth has an inclination and also the fact that the orbit of Earth around the Sun is not a perfect circle but an ellipse.

So the table shows that for Earth the rotation is 1 day, which is close enough to 24 hours. Earth is said to take 1 year to revolve around the Sun, or 365 days for all intents and purposes. Rocket science has to be much more precise than this but for our busy, everyday lives these approximations suffice.

Note that one day on Venus is quite long - approximately 243 of our days on Earth. That is, a day on Venus is almost 8 of our months! A "year" on Venus is approximately 224 of our Earth days, about seven and a half of our months.

In contrast, Mars is very different. A day on Mars is very close to a day on Earth, about 1.03 Earth days. This would be important if we were launching spacecraft towards the red planet but for all practical purposes we could say that Mars and Earth have a similar circadian rhythm of approximately 24 hours. However, its revolution around the Sun takes 1.88 of our year. So Mars takes longer to go round our Sun and therefore has a longer year.

From this illustration, we see that even within our Solar system, the planets have different days and years. We could draw a table to include all the planets in our system including the very large planets. If Mars and Venus represent any of the higher worlds described in the Buddhist texts, then we understand that our terrestrial longevity can be compared with other cycles not just within our solar system but also outside of our system.

Planet	Rotation	Revolution
Jupiter	9 hrs 51 minutes	11.86 earth years
Saturn	10 hrs 39 mins	29.46 earth years
Uranus	17 hrs 14 mins	164.79 earth years
Neptune	17.03 hours	164.79 earth years
Pluto	6.3867 earth days	247.69 earth years

[Table 5]

We see, from the above tables, that just within our solar system there is a great variation in rotation rates of the planets around their own axes, as well as their revolutionary rates of orbit around the Sun. Time is flexible.

Strictly speaking, the term *planets* refers to worlds within our Solar System. It is derived from the word *planetes*, meaning "wanderers". Ancient observers of the night sky noticed that the Moon and worlds within our solar system moved against the backdrop of apparently fixed stars - because they are closer to us.

Our science has now identified well over 4,100 worlds outside our solar system, known as exo-planets. These are of varying sizes and have different revolutionary orbits around their Suns and no doubt have different rates of rotation around their own axes as well as different conditions, some of which may not be suitable for life "as we know it".

The Buddha said:

"Monks, as far as sun and moon revolve and illuminate all directions by their radiance, so far does the thousand-fold world system extend.
And in that thousand-fold world system, there are a thousand moons, a thousand suns, a thousand Sinerus - kings of mountains,
a thousand Rose-Apple continents,
a thousand Western Goyana continents,
a thousand Northern Kuru continents,
a thousand Eastern Videha continents.
A thousand four great oceans,
a thousand Four Great Divine Kings and their heavens,
a thousandfold of the heavens of the Thirty-three Gods,

of the Yama Gods,
of the Tusita Gods,
of the Gods of Creative Joy,
of the gods controlling other's Creations
and there are a thousand Brahma worlds.
"As far O monks, as this thousand-fold world-system extends, the Great Brahma ranks there as the highest. But even for the Great Brahma, change takes place, transformation takes place."

(Anguttara Nikaya, X.29)

Ten fetters and four paths

There are five lower fetters that can bind beings to Kama loka. These are self-delusion, sceptical doubt, dependence on belief in efficacy of mere right and ritual, sensuality and ill-well.

Five upper fetters that bind beings to the two higher spheres are conceit, arrogance, self-assertion, personality, restless character, nescience and uknowing - ignorance, as well as desire for those higher planes.

CHAPTER 4

Longevity and Epochs

The Buddha stated that there was an epoch, a long time ago when humanity's life-span was 60,000 years. He said that in those days there lived a religious teacher named Araka.

"Long ago, O monks, there lived a religious teacher and founder of a creed, by name of Araka, who was free of sensual lust. He had many hundreds of disciples and this was the doctrine he taught to them: "Short is the life of man, O brahmans, limited and brief; it is full of suffering, full of tribulation. This, one should wisely understand, should do good and live a pure life; for none who is born can escape death..... Just as a dew-drop on the tip of a blade of grass will quickly vanish at sunrise and will not last long: even so, is man's life like a dew-drop. It is short, limited and brief. It is full of suffering, full of tribulation.""

Whilst endorsing Araka's teaching, the Buddha says:

"But nowadays O monks, one could rightly say, "Short is the life of man....." Because nowadays, he who lives long, lives for a hundred years or a little more."

(Anguttara Nikaya, VII.70)

The Buddha indicated that there may have been a time, a Cosmic period long gone, when humans had a much longer life-span than a mere hundred years. The lesson here is that time awareness is relative. What may seem inconceivable ages to us, may be just a fraction of time for other races elsewhere in our vast, mind-boggling Universe. Space and time appear to be endless - do we live in an eternal now and is our spot of consciousness the central pin-point of an infinite space? The Buddha himself spoke of these cosmic cycles, these aeons, these *kalpas*. Once, having recalled one of his previous lives in ages gone by, he told his monks:

"**For seven years I cultivated thoughts of loving-kindness *(metta or maitreya)*. Having cultivated a heart full of maitreya for seven years, I did not return to this sphere (kama-loka) for seven cyclic aeons of world-destructions and world originations. Whenever a world was destroyed, I entered (by way of rebirth) the Realm of the Radiant Gods and when the world unfolded again, I was reborn in an empty Brahma palace. And there, I was the Great Brahma, the unvanquished victor, all-powerful. And thirty-six times I was Sakka, Ruler of Gods, and many hundred times I was a world-ruling king - a just and righteous king......"**

(Anguttara Nikaya, VII.58)

The life-span on the World of Radiant Brahmas (Abode type Number 17 - see Table) is said to be 8 maha-kalpas, 8 great aeons. A maha-kalpa is vaguely defined as the time required to empty a certain volume filled with mustard seeds by disposing of one seed every hundred years. If that does not satisfy the yearning of a scholar, there is an alternative one: a maha-kalpa equals four incalculable aeons. One incalculable aeon is said to equal twenty cycles appertaining to the world. The conclusion is that there is no definitive time period assigned to an aeon in terms of the age of Earth, or the colossal age of the Solar system, or indeed the age of our Galaxy, the Milky Way.

The Buddha stated definitively:

"Undetermined monks, is the beginning of the world. The past extremity of beings, running on in birth after birth, bound by ignorance and the bonds of craving, is not manifest."
(Samyutta Nikaya, II.178)

Abode-type 27, the World of Supreme Brahmas, is said to have beings with a longevity of 16,000 maha-kalpas. In contrast, the Buddha says:

"Just as a line drawn on water with a stick will quickly vanish and will not last long,

even so is man's life like a line drawn on water. It is short!"
(Anguttara Nikaya, VII.70)

In the same discourse, the Buddha pleads with his followers not to waste time:

"Here O monks are trees, here are empty dwellings. Meditate O monks. Be not negligent, lest you feel regret later!"

The 27 types of abode described in Buddhist cosmology are said not to be seen as forever and forever. In Buddhist teaching, everything in manifestation is in a state of flux, is ever changing, therefore not static. So the classification of the 27 levels is also subject to change. The supramundane levels of consciousness and their related world-types, beyond the 27 levels already described will be studied in the next part of this anthology.

That "change" is embodied in all manifestation is an important lesson, for scientists and non-scientists alike, to grasp as a fundamental fact within the exquisite framework that forms the universe, both seen and unseen.

The Lord Buddha made an important declaration about change, about life, about the many levels of consciousness to be found through the cosmos, thus:

"There will be a time, O monks, when this world will come to an end. And at that time, beings are generally reborn in the Heaven of Radiant Deities. There they live, made of mind, feeding on joy, radiating light from themselves, traversing the skies, living in glory and thus they remain for a very long time. When the world comes to an end, O monks, these Radiant Deities rank as the highest but even for the Radiant Brahmas, change takes place, transformation takes place".

(Anguttara Nikaya, X.29)

<u>To repeat:</u>

**"Made of mind,
"Feeding on joy,
"Radiating light from themselves,
"Traversing the skies,
"Living in glory."**

Millennia before the advent of modern science, the Buddha had described the splendour in the variety of life forms in the cosmos.

The latter part of that discourse goes on to say:

"But even for the Radiant Brahmas (abbhassara deva), change takes place, transformation takes place. When seeing this O monks, a well-taught noble disciple is repelled by it; being repelled by it, he becomes disenchanted about the highest, not to speak of what is low."

It may seem very odd that the Buddha spoke of disenchantment with high and low. The crux of his message was the *fact of impermanence.* When a human mind realises the truth of constant, universal change, disenchantment may reinforce the idea that whatever is constantly changing cannot really be a source of satisfaction; therefore there can arise a yearning for the realisation of something more lasting, more durable - like an Absolute Reality, Nirvana.

This leads us to contemplate on what is manifest and what is not. Science postulates a "Big Bang Theory". Science suggests that at a moment in time, way back when, the universe came into being as a result of a "big bang". In other words, according to science, manifestation first occurred approximately 13.8 billion years ago. And within this manifestation are all observable phenomena.

The Buddha stated:

"Monks, there is an unborn, unoriginated, unmade, unformed. Were there not such a state, there would be no escape from what is born, originated, made, formed. Since monks, there *is* such a state, there is an escape from the born, originated, made and formed."

(Udana, p 80)

So the Buddha reminded the world that it is possible to escape from the wheel of birth, death and rebirth by the cessation of craving and attachment - towards the goal of Absolute Reality (Nirvana). He said:

"Thus, O monks, before my Enlightenment, when I was still an unenlightened Bodhisatta, being myself subject to the nature of birth, old age, sickness, death, sorrow and defilement, I sought after these things. Then I thought why, being myself subject to the nature of birth, old age, sickness, death, sorrow and defilement do I seek after these things? Suppose being myself subject to these things, seeing danger in them, I sought after the unborn, unageing, unailing, deathless, sorrowless, undefiled supreme peace, surcease of bondage - Nibbana."

(Majjhima Nikaya)

Here again, the Buddha declares that there is an Absolute Reality, beyond all manifestation.

The Happy Celestial abodes (the Deva Lokas within the bottom Sphere), as well as the four Jhana planes, constituting the Fine-Material Sphere (the Rupa Loka) and its sixteen Brahma worlds are regarded as places of abode as well as mental states of consciousness - because both are possible.

Although we are bound by gravity to this Earth, our civilisation has managed through rocket science to escape gravity and send probes to other planets in our Solar System and beyond.

So we may ultimately be space travellers but are still part of, originally - our Gaia, Mother Earth. Even if we succeed in terraforming other planets and start inhabitations elsewhere, we are still terrestrials. Unless humanity originated from outside Earth, Terra.

So indeed, even those sentient life-streams that "traverse the skies" and "live in glory" may be part of an abode, with its corresponding level of consciousness.

To remind ourselves of what the Buddha said:

"Made of mind,
"Feeding on joy,
"Radiating light from themselves,
"Traversing the skies,
"Living in glory."

Made of mind

What is mind? Dictionaries state:

"The mind is the set of cognitive faculties including consciousness, imagination, perception, thinking, judgement, language and memory, which is housed in the brain. It is usually defined as the faculty of an entity's thoughts and consciousness."

The entire nervous system, including the spine should be defined as part of the brain and therefore a broad network which houses "mind" as a focal point of consciousness. The functions of the brain, sense organs and nervous system are ultimately applied to and understood by the consciousness of an individual.

When the Buddha said that beings in higher worlds are "made of mind", was he implying that it is possible to have bodies, or form, made of a subtle mind-substance? This is not an absurd idea. Many people throughout the world believe that we have subtle forms, often described in metaphysical literature as 'astral', 'etheric' or 'mental' bodies.

Scientific research into this possibility is ongoing so we cannot dismiss the idea. Cognitive and neuroscience may well provide answers to some of these difficult conceptual musings.

The question "What is mind?" can be juxtaposed with the question, "What is consciousness?"

Later in this book, we shall examine 'consciousness' as carefully defined in Buddhist psychology.

Feeding on joy

Now, here is a fascinating concept. The Buddha is stating that higher beings can be nourished by "joy". People who take joy in others achievements are known to live long and happy lives.

Feeding and metabolism require healthy diets, balanced with carbohydrates, proteins, vitamins, fats, essential minerals, fibrous substances and water.

Can one live without material food? Most human beings cannot do so and would perish in a short time. There have been claims that some yogis have been able to live without food or water for extended periods of time. Clearly, there is need for further careful research into these claims.

Most normal human beings can live without water for 4 days. There was a report on a TV programme called "Discovery Science" that Dr. Sudhir V. Shah, a Director of Neurosciences at Ahmedabad investigated an Indian holy man by the name of Prahlad Jani, who was kept under observation for 10 days in a clinical study. Jani claims that he has not eaten since the age of 12 years and the study found that did not eat or drink for ten days while he was under close observation. Dr. Shah concluded that Jani was living off energy directly from the Sun. A controversial theory for certain - one that medical science will have to come to grips with in the future.

Is "joy" an energy from the Sun? Are the Sun's radiations "pure love" - *maitreya*? There certainly would not be any life on Earth without the Sun's radiation. The life in the seas and oceans is regulated by the Moon causing the ebb and tide of the waters, which in turn has a bearing on life on land and in the oceans. So the whole Sun-Earth-Moon system is a complex interplay of magnetic energies within the solar system, with the planets upholding life and allowing evolution on all the known worlds.

Our Sun, 864,000 miles in diameter, radiates energies twenty-four hours per day. The combination of energies, from cosmic rays to heat, ultraviolet rays and infrared wavelengths add up to life-giving and life-sustaining beams that shine out into space in all directions.

"Ah, happily do we dwell, owning nothing; We shall live on joy itself, like the Radiant Gods."
Dhammapada 200

Radiating light from themselves

As stated earlier, the word *deva* is derived from the word *div* meaning 'to shine'. Shining beings can radiate light from themselves. The Buddha stated, quite clearly that the shining beings from higher worlds radiate light from themselves. There is no suggestion here that they are reflecting light from an external source. They are radiating light from within themselves.

There have been reports of unidentified aerial objects, seemingly "structured craft" of some sort, landed on Earth with beings associated, moving around the craft, some of whom were shining.

Traversing the skies

In 1993, a mathematician named Richard L. Thompson, wrote and published a book entitled: **"Alien Identities - Ancient Insights into Modern UFO Phenomena"** in which he attempted to correlate many recent sightings of unidentified flying objects (UFOs) with *'vimanas'* - as described in eastern literature. Governments now refer to these objects as unidentified aerial vehicles (UAV).

Primarily, he quoted from the *Mahabharata* and the *Ramayana* and a later text from the 9th century A.D. known as the *Bhagavata Purana*.

The word *vimana* literally means "measuring out" or "having been measured out". It can also be defined as a self-moving aerial vehicle. The word also refers to "mansions". The Pushpaka Vimana of Ravana, as told in the *Ramayana* is said to be an example of an airborne vessel used to take an unwilling Sita to Lanka.

Some readers may smile with cynicism and remark that these ancient Indian works from the Vedic times are simply mythology and not to be taken as historical truth. One can debate as to what is "historical truth" and note that history is quite often written from the perspective of biased human beings, especially in latter times.

In some Indian languages, vimana (or vimanam) means 'aircraft', as in the town name Vimanapura (a suburb of Bangalore) or Vimannagar, a town in Pune.

Vimanas fall into two classes:

(1) Manmade craft that look like aeroplanes and fly with visible wing-like structures like birds but with engines for motive power.

(2) Vehicles that fly in a mysterious manner and can take on many different shapes, without visible wings or engines. Such are described in ancient Vedic works such as the *Rg Veda,* the *Mahabharata,* the *Ramayana* and the *Puranas.*

The epic Vedic text the *Ramayana* recounts accounts of a vimanas. The paramount tale here is that long ago, a country on this Earth known as Lanka was occupied by a race of beings known as Raksasas. Be that as it may, the story is that Ravana, the king of the Raksasas abducted the princess Sita, who was the wife of Lord Rama, and held her in his fortified city. It is said that Ravana also had an aerial mansion, a vimana, that could fly at the command of his mental powers.

The story unfolds as follows: Lord Rama instructed Hanuman, an intelligent human-ape-like being to locate Sita. Hanuman was apparently the son of the wind-god Vayu and possessed mystical powers which he used to remote view Ravana's aerial mansion, which was hovering over the capital city of Lanka.

It is said that Hanuman, with the aid of many helpers built a stone bridge to get from India to Lanka. It is worth noting here that the crew of the Space Shuttle in 2010 photographed what appears to be submerged stones, creating what is now an underwater link between India and Sri Lanka, reported to be 1.7 million years old. This has been called Rama Setu, referred by some as Adam's Bridge.

Vimana vatthu

The Buddhist text, *Vimana Vatthu* part of the Khuddaka Nikaya is a collection of 83 stories in verse describing the vimana — a kind of personal heavenly mansion — inhabited by beings reborn as gods or goddesses (devata) as a reward for meritorious deeds performed by them as human beings. All the stories follow a similar pattern. They begin with an introductory verse (or verses) in which the god or goddess is asked about the cause for his or her rebirth within that particular mansion, or vimana. The deva thereupon relates his or her previous good deeds in these stories.

Even in modern Hindu schools, there is reference to other worlds. For example, in the book "Srimad Bhagavatam - Eleventh Canto - Part Two" written by A.C. Bhaktivedanta Swami Prabhupada, Founder-Acarya of the International Society for Krishna Consciousness, it says in Chapter 6:

"Many demigods, coming to the earth to assist Lord Krishna in His pastimes, took birth within the Yada dynasty and appeared as Lord Krishna's associates. When the Lord had completed His earthly pastimes He wanted to send these demigods back to their previous service in universal administration. **Each demigod was to return to his respective planet.**"

A reasonable question

If shining beings can propel themselves through space with the power of their mind, why would they need space vehicles? It may be that they need to carry instrumentation, mobile laboratories for scientific exploration and observation and other material objects for whatever purpose they are engaged in. There are many open-minded scientists who believe that our Galaxy is populated by extraterrestrial beings and that they must be engaged in widespread exploration and education of lower worlds by higher worlds. It may be that some races make warfare against others.

Living in glory

The simplest explanation is that beings are reborn on the worlds suited to their particular Karma (Kamma in Pali) which has accrued over innumerable past lives. The word Jhana (Dhyana in Sanskrit) as used in the Pali texts means 'mental absorptions', a measure of the *degree* of contemplative power and resultant ability.

A fuller understanding of the Jhana planes will emerge in this section as we continue upwards into the top Sphere of existence - the Formless Sphere (Arupa Loka). When the Buddha was asked whether he would, in the future become a man or a god, he replied: "neither".

"Just as a blue, red or white lotus, though born and grown in the water, rising above the water stands unsoiled by it, so though born and grown in the world, having overcome the world, I abide unsoiled by the world - consider me as a Buddha."

(Anguttara Nikaya, IV.36)

The word Buddha means "Enlightened One" or "Awakened One" and the inference here is that a fully enlightened being can rise above not just this world level but above all world levels, beyond the Formless Sphere into the supra-mundane levels of consciousness termed as "nirvana".

The acme of the Buddha's teaching was the road to release from the wheel of birth and death (samsara) into the *unconditioned* state of an absolute reality, attainable to those capable of the deepest meditation.

"Those wise ones, who are intent on meditation and who delight in the peace of renunciation - such mindful, perfect Buddhas, even the Devas hold most dear."

(DhammaPada, 14.3)

By way of a summary, as well as an extension of the gamut of Buddhist cosmology, let us remind ourselves of the three spheres of existence:

Formless Sphere (the top sphere - Arupa Loka)

Fine-Material Sphere (Rupa Loka, wherein life still retains a form is the middle sphere)

Sense-Desire Sphere (bottom sphere, wherein human existence finds itself - Kama Loka)

World types in the top sphere, 28, 29, 30 and 31 relate to the 5th, 6th, 7th and 8th Jhanas respectively. The Pali word 'jhana' is derived from a root word meaning 'to think'. Mental absorption is supposed to result from intense concentration, so intense that it can burn out adverse hindrances that might stand in the way of successful contemplation.

The four world-types in the Arupa Loka, or levels of consciousness arise as a result of meditation on the "Formless" (Arupa) say the Buddhist scriptures. At the highest level, consciousness is said to be so subtle that it is defined as "Neither Perception Nor Non-Perception, Level 31.

"There is no arising of consciousness without conditions" said the Buddha. Consciousness depends upon four of the five aggregates:

Matter (*rupa khanda*)
Sensations (*vedana khandha*)
Perceptions (*sanna khandha)*
Mental formations (*samkhara khandha*)

The fifth aggregate is consciousness itself (*vinnana khandha).*

By now the reader will have gathered that the word *khandha* stands for 'aggregate'.

CHAPTER 5 - The Formless Sphere

	THE FORMLESS SPHERE (ARUPA LOKA)	
	Description	Jhana plane
31	Neither Perception Nor Non-Perception	8
30	Realisation Of The Void (Nothingness)	7
29	Infinity Of Consciousness	6
28	Infinity Of Space	5

[Table 5]

It is difficult for us to imagine, or even fully understand such worlds with their levels of high consciousness. Within our everyday lives, our small consciousness is tied to our physical bodies making us identify our minds with our material bodies, perhaps except during the sleep state or temporary states of unconsciousness, or NDE - near-death experiences or at the point of death.

Those spiritual aspirants who develop *jhanas* on Earth, are presumed to be reborn on the Arupa or the lower Rupa loka planes.

Beings in the Formless Arupa Loka are said to possess consciousness, albeit a very high level but possess no "material form" - that is no body of a dense physical nature.

Beings in the Rupa Loka possess consciousness as well as subtle bodies, with the exception of Level 22, a special type of world where beings are said to have a material body but their consciousness is held in a temporary state of suspension, for karmic reasons.

Beings in the Deva Lokas of the Sense-Desire Sphere (Kama Loka) also have subtler bodies than those of humans. It is possible that humans also have subtle bodies but are not aware of them in general. unless they develop psychic powers in their lifetime.

A dialogue between the Lord Buddha and one of his prominent monks was recorded as follows:

"Once the Venerable Ananda approached the Blessed One and asked: "Can it be O Lord that a monk attains to such a concentration of mind, that in Earth he is not conscious of Earth, nor in water is he conscious of water, nor in fire............wind, the realms of infinite space, of infinite consciousness, of nothingness, of 'neither-perception-nor-non-perception', is he conscious of this world or a world beyond - but yet he is conscious?"

The Buddha replied:

"Yes Ananda, there can be such a concentration of mind, that in Earth........., - but yet he is conscious."

(The preceding is repeated in full, in the original text.)

Ananda asks: "But how Lord can a monk attain to such a concentration of mind?"

"Herein Ananda, the monk is thus conscious: this is the peaceful, this is the best, namely the stilling of all karma

formations, the forsaking of all substrata (of rebirth), the elimination of craving, detachment, cessation - Nirvana. In that way Ananda, may a monk attain to such a concentration of mind."

(Anguttara Nikaya, X.7)

Nirvana, the ultimate goal in Buddhist striving, is known as the only Absolute Reality in the religion. This Sanskrit word is derived from "ni" and "vana". The equivalent Pali word is "nibbana".

"Ni" implies negation, "vana" means craving. Thus, the word Nirvana is defined as the negation of all craving. It is craving, said the Buddha that weaves the web of suffering, delicately entwining the strands of karma upon the manifestation of mind and bodily matter.

"I declare, monks, that actions (karma) willed, performed and accumulated, will not become extinct as long as their results have not been experienced, be it in this life, in the next life, or in future lives. And as long as these results of actions willed, performed and accumulated, have not been experienced, there will be no end to suffering, I declare."

(Anguttara Nikaya, X.206)

Nirvana is taught to be supramundane consciousness, beyond and above the Formless Sphere (Arupa Loka). It is said to be an objective, blissful state which is deathless, non-conditioned, incomparable and endless.

Time is also part of manifestation, therefore past, present and future are divisions of relativity, not existent in reality - as reality is the one unchangeable. So time cannot limit or condition Nirvana in any way.

The Buddha said:

"Birth is suffering, old age, sickness, death, sorrow, lamentation, pain, grief and despair are suffering, not to get what one wishes is suffering.......
"And what monks, is the conditioned origin of suffering ....craving!
"And what, monks is the cessation of suffering? Through the cessation of craving, there is cessation of suffering"

(Anguttara Nikaya, VI.63)

A fully enlightened being, such as the Buddha, is said to possess many different kinds of supernormal powers and knowledge. These include variegated psychic powers, the Celestial Ear, the ability to discern others' thoughts, the reminiscence of past births and lives and the all-seeing Celestial Eye.

The Buddha was once asked how far his voice would reach in the Universe. He replied that enlightened ones were immeasurable and could reach **"further than a thousand-fold world-system"**; even further than a three-thousand-fold world-system. They could penetrate all those worlds with their shining splendour and reach all living beings there, with their voice. There is more than one story in the texts, of the Buddha disappearing from one spot and reappearing in another, as speedily as **"A strong man might stretch his bent arm or bend his stretched arm"**.

It is a belief in Buddhism that the process of rebirth can also be spontaneous, not necessarily by conception in a womb. The texts state that reproduction on the higher types of world is non-sexual in nature and is by spontaneous rebirth (*opapatika* in the Pali language). The exact mechanism has not been described in detail. The author has seen only one book which clearly and authoritatively explains rebirth on higher worlds and that is in "The Nine Freedoms" written by Dr. George

King, late Founder and President of the Aetherius Society.

Buddhists will say that some of the beings born spontaneously in the Deva Lokas of the Sense-Desire Sphere (Kama Loka) are asexual - neither male not female.

All beings born spontaneously in the Rupa Lokas of the Fine-Material Sphere (the Brahma worlds) are not only asexual but also devoid of the essence of the sense organs of nose and tongue. The sensitive material qualities of such sense organs are of little practical use to Brahmas who possess finer, more subtle senses and psychic powers. Although such organs may be present in their Fine-Material bodies, their function would be superfluous.

Life-forms in the Formless Sphere (Arupa Loka) do not retain any physical form of sense-organs because they are essentially made of mind, at the four highest levels. For us on Earth, it would be difficult to imagine their true nature and capabilities.

"The Enlightened One recollects his manifold past lives; that is to say: one birth, two births, three births, four births, five births, ten births, twenty births, thirty births, forty births, fifty births, a hundred births, a thousand births, a hundred thousand births.
Many aeons of world contraction, many aeons of world expansion, many aeons of world contraction and expansion.
There he was so named, of such a race, with such an appearance, such kind of food, such experience of pleasure and pain, such an end of his lifespan; and passing away from there, he reappeared here; thus with its aspects and particulars, he recollects his manifold past lives.........."

(Anguttara Nikaya, X.21)

In the same discourse, the Buddha continued:

"And again, with the Divine Eye, which is purified and surpasses the human, the Enlightened One sees beings passing away and reappearing, inferior and superior, fair and ugly, happy or unhappy in their destiny. He understands beings as *faring according to their deeds*."

The principle of "faring according to one's deeds" is a very practical way of understanding the Law of Karma and the fruits of individual karma.

The first precept undertaken by all Buddhists is to 'not kill'. A similar belief exists in other religions, yet this precept is broken very often throughout the world.

"The taking of life, O monks, I declare to be threefold: as caused by greed, caused by hate, caused by delusion...............So also the taking of what is not given, sensual misconduct, lying, tale-bearing, harsh speech, vain talk, covetousness, ill-will. Wrong views too, I declare to be threefold: as caused by hate and greed, caused by delusion.
"Hence monks, greed is a producer of Karmic concatenation, delusion is a producer of Karmic concatenation. But by

the destruction of greed, hate and delusion - there is exhaustion of Karmic concatenation."

(Anguttara Nikaya, X.174)

The Buddha defined right views and correct ideas in the following manner:

"There is moral value in gifts, offerings and sacrifice; there is fruit and recompense from deeds good or evil; there is both this world and another world; there are duties towards mother and father;

"There exist spontaneously-mind-born beings and there exist in this world recluses: living and conducting themselves rightly, who can explain this world and the worlds beyond, having realised them by their own direct knowledge."

(Anguttara Nikaya, X.206)

In the above discourse, the Buddha is self-referencing on the knowledge he obtained in his deep meditations; knowledge about the world systems and our place in the cosmos. At the same time he is delivering a short sermon with a code of ethics and moral behaviour for humanity to succeed in living right.

The development of psychic powers is not the "be-all and end-all" of Buddhism. Rather - such powers are a natural by-product of spiritual advancement and have to be controlled and used strictly within the divine Law of Karma. Any irresponsible display of psychic powers is frowned upon by Buddhist monks. The development of the higher states of meditation is seen as the path to enlightenment and release from the Wheel of birth and death, through the elevated states of the eight Jhana planes into that Absolute Reality which is termed Nirvana.
The Buddha once said of himself:

"To the Enlightened One, when asked about touching the Path which leads to the World of Brahma, there can be neither doubt nor difficulty. For Brahma I know.

And the world of Brahma and the path which leadeth unto it, yes I know it - even as one who has entered the Brahma world and has been born within it.

(Tevijja Sutta, Digha Nikaya, 38)

This famous sutra, "Tevijja Sutra" was given to "knowers of the Three Vedas". The religion practised in India at the time of the Buddha was Brahminism, based on the ancient Vedas, of which there are three, although there are four today because of a later addition to the Vedas.

So the "Tevijja Sutra" opened the eyes of those who were well-versed in the Three Vedas because the Buddha was also educated into and knowledgeable about the Vedas and went further than the Vedas, in his teaching, based on his own meditative experiences.

Drawing on his skill as an archer, the Buddha said:

"Even if one moves with the swiftness of an arrow, in any direction, travelling for a

whole lifetime, one cannot hope to reach the limits of space."

Our study has shown the Buddhist overview of the Cosmos, the mental and meditative levels of realisation and the unchangeability of an Absolute Reality, which lies beyond all the Jhana planes.

As far as the age of the Universe and evolution of life within its endless boundaries (which modern scientists calculate from a supposed "Big Bang Theory" to be over thirteen billion years) the Buddha stated:

"There are four incalculable epochs, monks. The four are: the Enveloping Epoch, the Enveloped Epoch, the Developing Epoch, the Developed Epoch. The epoch during which there is cosmic envelopment is not easy to reckon as so many years or centuries or tens of hundreds of centuries."

(Anguttara Nikaya, IV.156)

Buddhists believe that the succession of Great Kalpas, the cycles of cosmic evolution and dissolution, which envelop the lesser kalpas of world-systems is endless.

Buddhist tradition has it that the present wotld-period is a fortunate one, as five Buddhas are destined to appear in it. Since the fourth one, the Gautama Buddha has already been and left, Buddhists expect the next Enlightened One in the future to be the Maitreya Buddha.

The Sanskrit word *maitreya* means the same as the Pali word *metta* and is gracefully translated as loving-kindness. It also means benevolence, goodwill, friendliness and in a compassionate sense is the wish for the happiness of all beings, without exception to creed, class or faith.

The appearance of Buddhas within a single kalpa is said to be separated by cataclysmic changes which ruin cultural continuity, such that the characteristic teaching of all Buddhas (the Four Noble Truths) is lost to the Age and the subsequent Buddha, after rebirth on Earth from a higher plane, has to rediscover the Eightfold Path by its own efforts.

The deeper Buddhist philosophy deals with 121 types of consciousness, 52 mental states, thought-processes and several psychic powers in the course of a human lifetime and at rebirth, one of the 31 abodes as described in this study. The minute classification of *karma*, action and its resultants is an encyclopaedic branch of Buddhism.

The boundaries between the human world (in the Sense-Desire Sphere) and those immediately above it are not so rigid as to be insurmountable. Lines of communication are possible, although the higher types of world would require a correspondingly higher level of Samadhic meditative ability in order to form contact with shining beings.

Once while sitting in a simpsasa grove, the Buddha compared the number of simsapa leaves he was clutching in his hand, to the number of leaves left in the tree, with the following simile:

"Such is the comparison between the Truths I have realised and revealed to you and those which I have not revealed."

[The simsapa tree has been identified as either *Dalbergia sissoo*, a rosewood tree common to India and southeast Asia, or *Amherstia nobilis*, another South Asian tree, of the family *Caesalpiniaceae*.]

The Buddha advocated true speech always. The power of Truth and One who always speaks truth is best epitomised by his assertion:

"Monks, whatever a Buddha [an Enlightend One] speaks, utters and proclaims, from the day of His Full Enlightenment up to the day when he finally passes away into the Nirvana element that is without a residue of the five groups of clinging - all that is just so and not otherwise."

Anguttara Nikaya, Book of Fours)

It is time to review all 31 levels:

THE THREE SPHERES OF EXISTENCE

31 Sphere of neither perception nor non-perception
30 Knowledge of nothingness (void)
29 Infinity of consciousness
28 Infinity of space **ARUPA LOKA**

===

27 Supreme Brahmas
26 Clear-sighted Brahmas
25 Beautiful Brahmas
24 Serene Brahmas
23 Immobile Brahmas
22 Sensationless Brahmas
21 Greatly Rewarded Brahmas
20 Brahmas of Steady Aura   Pure Brahma Worlds

----

19 Brahmas of Infinite Aura
18 Brahmas of Minor Aura
17 Radiant Brahmas
16 Brahmas of Infinite Lustre
15 Brahmas of Minor Lustre
14 Great Brahmas
13 Ministers of Brahma
12 Retinue of Brahma   Lower Brahma Worlds
                                   RUPA LOKA

===

11 Devas enjoying the creation of others
10 Devas enjoying their own creations
9 Tusita realms
8 Yama Devas
7 Realm of the 33 Devas
6 Realm of the Four Great Kings of the Four Quarters
5 The Human World
4 Animal realms
3 Unhappy "spirits"
2 Demons
1 Inferno or hells   **KAMA LOKA**

===

Above these three spheres of existence is said to lie "Lokuttara" - supramundane. The three spheres of existence on the other hand are known as mundane.

The Five Aggregates

The Buddha said that in manifestation, a "sentient being" consists of five aggregates (*skandha*):

Matter (rupa)
Feeling (vedana)
Perception (sanna)
Mental States (sankhara)
Consciousness (vinnana)

As we have already stated, the fifth one depends upon the other four.

Before we embark on a journey to understanding the classes and types of the five aggregates, as defined in Buddhist philosophy, it is worth noting that the Buddha burst the bubble of thinking that "appearance", in the world of mundane reality, is not deceptive, by also saying:

"Suppose that a man who is not blind, were to behold the many bubbles on the river Ganges, as they are driving along; and he should watch them and carefully examine them. After carefully examining them, however, they will appear to him empty, unreal and unsubstantial. In exactly the same way does the monk behold all the corporeal phenomena.... feelings.... perceptions... mental formations... states of consciousness, whether they be of the past, present or future.... far or near. And he watches them and examines them carefully and after carefully examining them, they appear to him, empty, unreal and unsubstantial."

Samyutta Nikaya (XXII, 95)

So, with the proviso that ultimately Absolute Reality is unmanifest, we can come down to Earth to study the five aggregates in the world of mundane reality.

There are 28 species of matter say the Buddhist texts. We have to be careful with the word "species" here, so as not to confuse the modern biological classification of life as genus and species. Four of these are said to be underived and twenty-four derived, making the total of 28. There is no equivalent to modern scientific classification of matter as consisting of atoms (or even sub-atomic particles) combining to create molecules.

There are 5 classes of "feeling" and 6 classes of "perception". Notice the difference between "mental states" and "consciousness". There is said to be 50 different mental states and 89 kinds, or types, of "consciousness".

It would be best to tabulate these to make matters clearer. The table below shows the three spheres of existence, as well as the supra mundane levels above them, thus totalling four lofty spheres.

We are now familiar with the three spheres of existence: Kama loka, Rupa loka and Arupa loka. Let us also not forget the eight levels of supra mundane states of consciousness, which can be classed as *nirvanic* states.

THE 3 SPHERES plus eight Nirvanic levels	Thoughts leading to actions		Indeterminate or karmically neutral actions from thoughts	
Levels	Moral	Immoral	Resultant	Functional
Nirvanic Lokuttara (8 states)	Path moment [4]		Fruit moment [4]	
Arupa Loka Abodes	[4]		[4]	[4]
Rupa loka Abodes	[5]		[5]	[5]
Kama loka Abodes	[8]	[12]	[23]	[11]
Totals [89]	[21]	[12]	[36]	[20]

In the table above, the 31 types of abodes in Kama, Rupa and Arupa loka are shown, numbered from 1 - 31, in the first column.. The supramundane levels, of which 8 are defined as extremely high states of the deepest meditation, some kind of *"cosmic consciousness"* are said to be the final keys to liberation and escape from the wheel of birth and death.

Notice that immoral thoughts (and resultant immoral actions) do not arise in the Rupa, Arupa and Supramundane levels.

Buddhist psychology defines 12 types of immoral thoughts that can and do arise in the lowest types of abode - the Kama Loka.

[Reference the numbers within square brackets, totalled horizontally and vertically.]

So there are a total of 21 types of thoughts leading to moral actions, eight in the lowest sphere, five in the Arupa abodes and four in the Arupa (formless) types of world. In the nirvanic states of deep meditation there are

said to be four such moral thoughts leading to actions.
4 + 4 + 5 + 8 = 21

There are 12 types of thought that can lead to immoral actions; these only occur in the Kama Loka. Eight of these are rooted in attachment; two in aversion and two in ignorance.

There are a total of 36 'resultant' actions which fall into the category of indeterminate or karmically neutral and 20 which are functional.

So we see a total of 89 = 21 + 12 + 36 + 20 *types* of consciousness. Actually, the Manual of Abhidhamma by Narada Thera, identifies a total of 121. Remember that Buddhism classifies 'mental states' as being separate from 'types of consciousness', two of the five aggregates..

The Buddha said that there are ten kinds of evil which can be committed through thoughts, related words and subsequent actions.

DEEDS: Killing
Stealing
Sexual misconduct

WORDS: Lying
Slandering
Harsh speech
Vain talk

THOUGHTS: Covetousness
Hatred
False views

"Hatred is never appeased by hatred in this world; only by love - this is an eternal law"
                                        Dhammapada

Nibbana (nirvana) is said to be the ultimate reality, which is supramundane (lokuttara) and beyond the worlds of mind, body - form or formless - beyond the five aggregates. It is the only Dhamma which is not conditioned by any cause; thus it is considered to be eternal and is neither a cause or an effect.

A contemplation

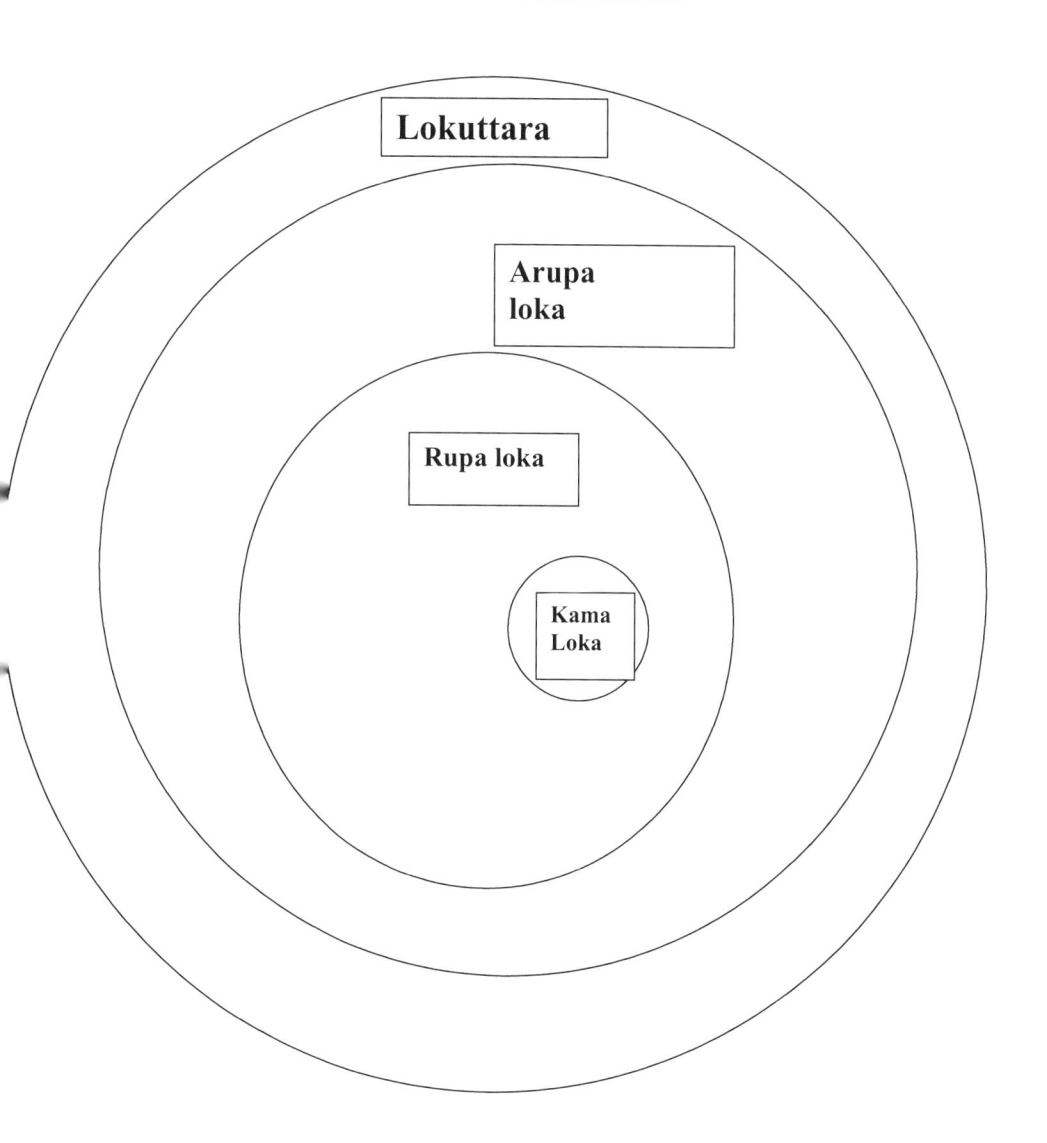

- Lokuttara
- Arupa loka
- Rupa loka
- Kama Loka

The Nine Freedoms

The author has read one book which has expanded on the levels of consciousness within our solar system, written by the English-born Yogi, Mystic and Founder of The Aetherius Society, Dr. George King.

The book is titled "THE NINE FREEDOMS, published in 1963 - and is highly recommended reading for all. The Aetherius Society also has a book of practice titled: "The Twelve Blessings", the text of which is actually a Cosmic Concept.

*Available from the Aetherius Society,
757 Fulham Road,
London, SW6 5UU
Telephone: +44 207 736 4187*

http://www.aetherius.org

OTHER WORLDS AND BUDDHISM - The Three Spheres of Existence

SQUARING THE CIRCLE

See the explanation on the next few pages for the numbers in brackets around the circle.

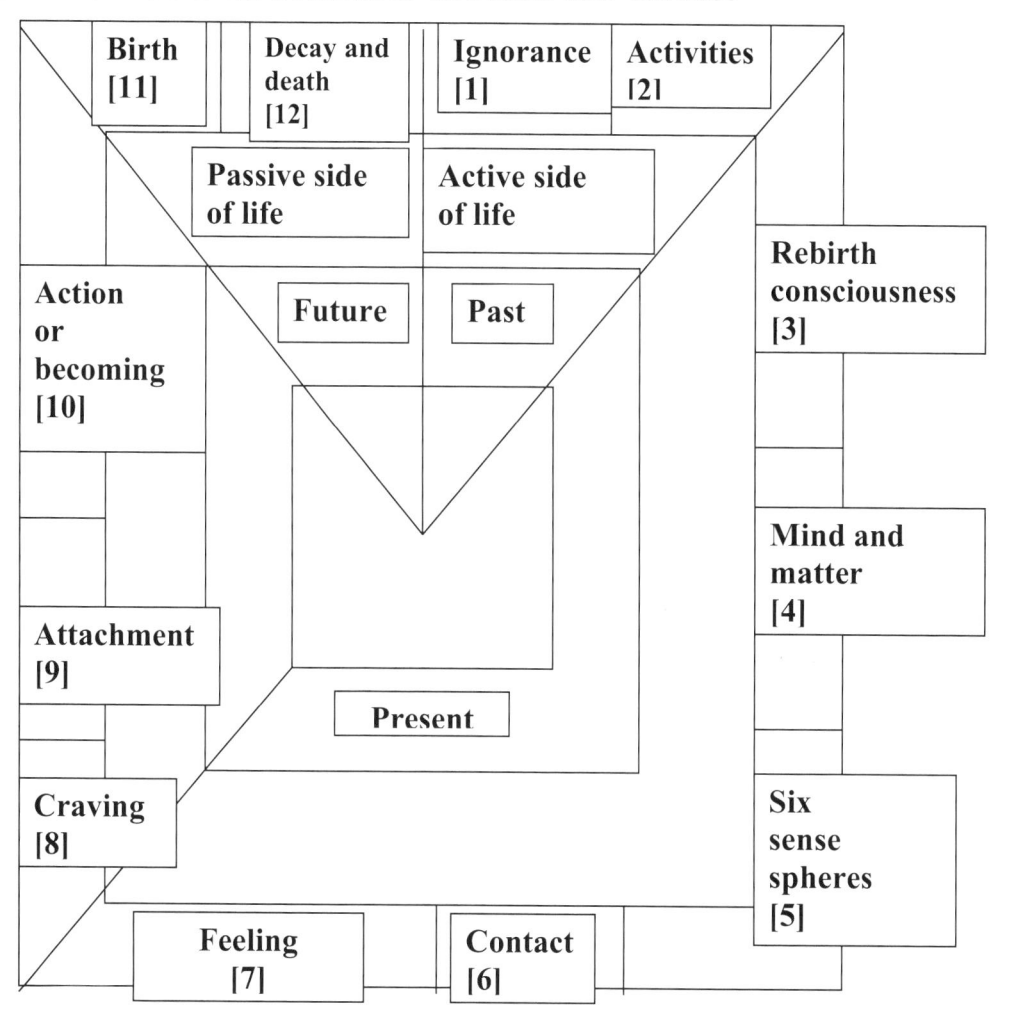

Birth [11]	Decay and death [12]	Ignorance [1]	Activities [2]

Passive side of life

Active side of life

Rebirth consciousness [3]

Action or becoming [10]

Future

Past

Mind and matter [4]

Attachment [9]

Present

Craving [8]

Six sense spheres [5]

Feeling [7]

Contact [6]

The Karmic wheel of birth, death and rebirth.
(Adapted from "A Manual of Abhidhamma")

Copyright ©Ananda L. Sirisena 2019

The "circle of life" diagram above explained:

[1] **Ignorance**. (*avijja*) The Buddha stated that the only sin is ignorance, i.e. of the karmic law, ignorance about the state of human sentience, ignorance about how to break away from the wheel of birth and rebirth. Not knowing the "Four Noble Truths".

[2] **Activities**. These activities are defined as
(a) craving (tanha), all types of craving no matter what philosophy they arise from.
(b) grasping (upadana), which gives rise to the false notion of "I" and "Mine".
(c) becoming (bhava) - moral and immoral action that conditions future birth.

Note that [1] and [2] are said to be arising as part of previous actions (kamma).

[3] **Rebirth-consciousness**. literally relinking consciousness. *(Patisandhi-vinnana)*. *Patisandhi* here refers to the initial thought-process that occurs at the moment of conception in a new birth (actually a rebirth).

[4] **Mind and matter**. *(Nama-Rupa)* Mind is known as *nama* and denotes both consciousness and mental states. *Rupa*, as we have defined before also stands for "form" or "shape" but in general refers to all "matter".

[5] **Six sense spheres.** *(Salyatana)*. The spheres where six senses operate, i.e. the five senses of eye, ear, nose, tongue, body and one of mind. It should be understood that all input from the five senses goes to the mind for neural analysis and comprehension. Body or skin gives rise to the sensation of 'touch'. The receptacle for all this sensory input is indeed the consciousness which can make sense of what is being detected.

[6] **Contact**. The Pali word for this is *phassa* The manual of AbhiDhamma states, "For any sense impression to occur, three things are essential - consciousness, respective sense and the object." The easy-to-understand example given in the manual is that one sees an object with the consciousness through the eye as its instrument. One can extend this example to the other four basic senses and their instruments: ear, nose, tongue and skin (for touch). Here

contact means 'it touches' but not in the feeling of 'touch' as in skin proximity. The manual states:
"It has 'touching' as its salient characteristic, impact as its function, coinciding as its manifestation and awareness as proximate cause."

[7] **Feeling** *(vedana)*. Feeling may be pleasurable, painful or neutral in its outcome. It is said to have no ethical importance unless it gives rise to immoral actions.

[3], [4], [5], [6] and [7] constitute parts of the present life. So do [8], [9] and [10].
[11] and [12] point to the future.
[1] and [2] are from the past.

[8] **Craving** *(tanha)*. The Abhidhamma manual states that craving is threefold:
(i) Craving for sensual pleasure (*kama-tanha*)
(ii) Craving for sensual pleasures with a belief in eternalism, thinking they are imperishable
(iii) Craving for sensual pleasures with the view of nihilism; i.e. with the belief that everything perishes after death - the materialistic point of view.

[9] **Attachment** (*upadana*). This is defined as intense craving resulting in an unhealthy attachment to one or more 'things'. It corresponds to the actual act of stealing and thought of possession with a false ego notion: e.g. "I own that object or person". The word *upadana* is an opposite to *dana* or giving, as in the kind thoughts of alms giving.

[10] **Action or becoming** (*bhava*). This is explained as both moral and immoral actions with karmic results through the three spheres of existence with the proviso, as we have seen earlier, that immoral actions (*akusala*) do not occur in the higher planes of Rupa, Arupa and Lokuttara.

[3],[4],[5],[6] and [7] are said to be part of the present but passive side of life.
[8],[9] and [10] are also said to be part of the present but active side of life.

[11] **Birth** (*jati*). This is a reference to the arising of the five aggregates on any of the planes or realms. It is of course a reference to our future birth as well. Both Buddhists and

Hindus do believe that liberation from the wheel of birth, death and rebirth takes many, many lives.

[12] **Decay and death** (*jara-marana*). This is a reminder, yet again, that life that is born must perish after some time. True for every cell in our own bodies, to our own lives, as well as the lives of all sentient beings and non-sentient life. This observation applies to single-celled organisms as well as to highly developed multi-celled creatures. It must apply as well to many different types of life outside of Earth too: "the two-footed, the no-footed, the four-footed, the many-footed".

The interval between birth and death is regarded as decay - however we can perceive that after birth *there is growth for some time* before ultimate death - and this fact is true for all living things.

To repeat: [1] and [2] relate to the past.
[11] and [12] are aspects of the future
All the other divisions of the circle constitute the present.

[8],[9] and [10] are features of the active side of life. The passive side of the present is shown by [3], [4], [5], [6] and [7].

Life on Mars

NASA, the The National Aeronautics and Space Administration, has struggled with the discovery of microbial life on Mars. The Viking lander experiments of 1976 apparently found evidence of microbes in the soil of Mars but the results were explained away as chemical reactions because the hierarchy at NASA did not want to accept as fact the possibility of microbial life on our neighbouring world. There had been a view held for many years that Mars was a dead world like our moon.

This reluctance to accept the reality of life outside Earth has been difficult to explain, as carefully examined in the book, "Mars - The Living Planet". It could be an adherence to medieval scriptures or simply an aversion to scientific facts - both examples of *upadana*.

A similar reluctance on the part of many scientists in mainstream science to studying, or accepting, that the many observations of unidentified aerial vehicles (uav or ufo) may be *vimanas* as described in the literature of the eastern religions.

Humanity stands at the threshold of a mental and spiritual renaissance which will open portals to other worlds and the understanding that in a huge galaxy we have never been alone, are not alone today and cannot be alone in the future.

May this brief voyage to other worlds as taught in Buddhism also enlighten the reader to the many forms of life we might encounter as we travel out in our space explorations.

There is hope for a peaceful world with interactions with other worlds - in peace.

The Buddha said:
"There is no net like delusion."

References and further reading

1). **"A Manual of Abhidhamma (An outline of Buddhist Philosophy)"** by Narada Maha Thera, 1956. Buddhist Publication Society, Kandy, Sri Lanka.

2). **"Buddhism and the Race Question"** by Dr. G.P. Malalsekera & K. N. Jayatilleke, UNESCO, 1958

3). **"Anguttara Nikaya" - Discourses of the Buddha".** Translated by Nyanaponika Thera

4). **"The Buddha On Meditation and Higher States of Consciousness"** by Daniel Coleman. Published by the Buddhist Publication Society.

5). **"Aspects of Reality as Taught by Theravada Buddhism"** by Dr. G.P. Malalsekera, 1968. Buddhist Publication Society, The Wheel Publication No. 127

6) **"Gods and the Universe in Buddhist Perspective"** by Francis Story, 1972. Buddhist Publication Society, The Wheel Publication No. 180/181

7) **"Discourses of the Buddha - Knowers Of Veda - Tevijja Sutta"** by T.W. Rhys Davids and Paul Debes., 1963/1977. Wheel Publication No. 57/58

8) **"Buddhist Ethics"** by Ven H. Saddhatissa, 1970. George Allen and Unwin Ltd.

9) **"The Nine Freedoms"** by Dr. George King, 1963. The Aetherius Society

10) **"What Is Nibbana?"** by Ven. H. Saddhatissa, 1984. Published by the British Mahabodhi Society.

11) **"Buddhism and the God-Idea"**, 1981. Nyanaponika Thera. The Wheel Publication No. 47, Buddhist Publication Society.

12) **"Alien Identities - Ancient Insights into Modern UFO Phenomena"** by Richard L. Thompson, 1993

13) **"UFOs - A Scientific Enquiry"** by J. Allen Hynek, 1980

14) **"The Flying Saucers - A Report on the Flying Saucers, Their Crews and Their Mission to Earth"** by Dr. George King. Aetherius Society 1964

15) **"UFOs - Generals, Pilots and Government Officials Go On The Record"** by Leslie Kean.
2010, Three Rivers Press

16) **"Psychic Exploration - A Challenge for Science"** by Edgar D. Mitchell, astronaut and sixth man to walk on the moon.
1974, G. P.Putnam's Sons, New York

17) **"Massive Vimana (UFO) Over The Atomic Weapons Establishment - A Challenge for Parliament"** by Ananda L. Sirisena
2014, available through Amazon Books

Printed in Great Britain
by Amazon